Swi   uois
for primary schools

Evans / Methuen Educational

*First published 1972 for the Schools Council
by Evans Brothers Limited
Montague House, Russell Square, London WC1B 5BX
and Methuen Educational Limited
11 New Fetter Lane, London EC4P 4EE*

*Distributed in the US by Citation Press
Scholastic Magazines Inc., 50 West 44th Street
New York, NY 10036*

SBN 423 86620 6

*Printed in Great Britain by
Richard Clay (The Chaucer Press) Ltd
Bungay, Suffolk*

Contents

PLATES
Four pages of photographs of different types of pools appear in the centre of the booklet.

Illustrations

The Schools Council and the publishers are grateful to the following for permission to reproduce illustrations: Greater London Council Photograph Library (plate 5); Mr John Hunt (plate 1); Purley Pools Limited (plates 4 and 8); Reading Local Education Authority (plate 6); Segment Swimming Pools Limited (plate 7).

Foreword

In 1970 a working party set up by the Physical Education Committee of the Schools Council carried out an inquiry into swimming in primary schools. They invited a large number of local education authorities in various parts of the country as well as institutions for physically handicapped children to describe their policies towards promoting swimming at primary-school level and their approaches to the various practical problems involved, including cost, choice of pools, maintenance, and teaching methods. They were asked to include, where possible, articles from headteachers and written comments by children.

The response was encouraging, and the many useful and stimulating replies received have been collated to form this report. The examples given of ways in which authorities and teachers have successfully met the challenge of providing swimming for large numbers of young children will, it is hoped, encourage others who have not so far felt able to develop this part of the curriculum to look again at the possibilities open to them.

In the short space available, it has not been possible to include quotations from every one of the replies received, especially as many, inevitably, made the same point. Exclusion does not imply lack of interest, merely lack of space.

The Schools Council is grateful to Mrs Jo Klein for all her work in writing this report.

Acknowledgements

The working party is grateful to the following authorities and special schools for their help with this inquiry:

Bedford; Bromley; Bristol; Buckinghamshire; Cambridgeshire and Isle of Ely; Cumberland; Derbyshire; Devon; Yorkshire (East Riding); East Suffolk; Essex; Essex (Harlow division); Halifax; Hampshire; Hertfordshire; Lincolnshire (parts of Holland); Inner London; Kent; Kingston-upon-Hull; Lincolnshire (parts of Lindsey); Newport, Mon.; Norfolk; Yorkshire (North Riding); Nottingham; Plymouth; Reading; Rutland; Scunthorpe; Somerset; Southend-on-Sea; Surrey; Teesside; West Suffolk; Wolverhampton; Worcestershire.

Dr Barnardo's Princess Margaret School, Taunton, Somerset; Florence Treloar School, Holybourne, Hampshire; Percy Hedley School, Newcastle-upon-Tyne; The Spastics Society's Meldreth Manor School, Hertfordshire.

I. Swimming and education

In England and Wales today there is widespread support for the principle of teaching every child to swim as a basic part of his education. Public opinion has also moved firmly towards the belief that, in practice, swimming ought to begin as early as possible: ideally, in the first years of primary schooling. As was stated in the Plowden Report:* '. . . we believe that the first priority is rightly placed on teaching the highest possible numbers of young children to gain confidence in water and to swim . . .'

Where primary-school swimming programmes have been expanded to meet this priority, local education authorities and headteachers speak with great enthusiasm of the way confidence gained in the swimming pool spills over into the classroom. A chief education officer reports that:

> Some heads were sceptical at first, but later have not regretted the time and energy required to include a swimming programme in their school curriculum. In encouraging this expanding programme . . . they frequently comment that, apart from the obvious advantages of enjoyment and survival, children have found a new confidence in their approach and general attitude to school work as a direct result of having learnt to swim . . .

The headmistress of a school where a pool was opened more than twelve years ago listed the benefits as follows:

> Swimming is one of the few activities that a child can take part in as a member of a family all his life, with his parents and then later on with his own children . . . Swimming gives some children a chance to shine . . . A child who is not built to run or jump is very often built to be a swimmer and this gives such a child a great sense of achievement. Also a child who is not academically brilliant may be able to swim, and such is the feeling of achievement that I have known cases of difficult children having a quite different attitude to school after having achieved success in swimming.

> Swimming is unique in that it provides relaxation of tension. All

* *Children and their Primary Schools*: a report of the Central Advisory Council for Education (England), (HMSO, 1967).

children feel tension to a greater or lesser degree in school but the changed element – water – seems to release these tensions . . . Also, swimming instruction is based on relaxation, an art which all human beings need to cultivate . . .

For children suffering from a physical or mental handicap, the beneficial effects of swimming are widely acknowledged. 'It is one form of sport where, whatever the disabilities, all are on an equal footing', wrote a physio-therapist from a school whose pupils are spastics or children suffering from muscular dystrophy, cerebral palsy, or spina bifida; all are encouraged to swim regularly.

The idea that swimming is of specific therapeutic value for such children was discounted by the principal of another special school, but he added, 'Our children benefit from exercise in the water, as do all children. Many non-ambulant children are able to move freely in water given suitable support. This is a very stimulating experience for them as they can more nearly approach normality . . . It has also been noted on many occasions that speech is stimulated. There are many valuable opportunities for incidental language training.' Another headmaster spoke of a boy with a pronounced speech defect who, since learning to swim, 'now talks volubly, and the progress he has made academically since his swimming success is remarkable'. In his experience, the effect of swimming on retarded children has been particularly noticeable: 'I could show you the exact day on which one girl realised she could swim just by looking at her school books.' The physically handicapped 'are so delighted with their success that they make better progress than one would have thought possible'.

What the children say
Not unexpectedly, the children's essays included in replies were full of praise for swimming lessons. The following extracts echo some of the points made earlier in this section by administrators and headteachers about the way in which swimming helps to build up the store of confidence that most pupils need.

> I like swimming because I am not a very good runner or in the school football team but I can swim better than many other boys.

.   .   .   .

When I go swimming I feel I am really enjoying myself getting away
from English and sums.

.   .   .   .

Children screaming, laughing, playing, splashing
In the cool blue water.
Just forget them, forget the heat,
Jump into the pool and dive beneath.

Suddenly silence, nothing moves or speaks,
You're cut off from the outside world,
And free to swim wherever you please.

How you wish you could stay forever
In the silent worlds of the water
Gliding like a fish in a carefree manner.

But then you feel that deepdown feeling
Crunching up your lungs and then you have to surface.
Leaving your adventures before they've begun.

.   .   .   .

The pool gives me freedom of movement and I can work muscles
which I never even move in my chair. For instance I have to use the
muscles of my legs to get me from place to place in the pool, whereas
on dry land I can scarcely bend them . . . When I first started swimming I could not swim without a ring; to tell the truth I did not have
the confidence . . . This was until one day when I was taken out of
my ring and put on my back. I was scared to death but this happened
several times and eventually I was ready to take my first badge for
which I had to swim two lengths of the pool, put my head under
water and retrieve a ball from six yards. A few months later I learned
to swim upright and I passed the next badge with ease having dived
in from the side . . .

(Boy aged 15, with muscular dystrophy)

II. Where children swim

Progress in learning to swim depends on many factors. These include the quality of teaching, the age when learning starts, and the frequency of lessons. All these factors are in turn greatly influenced by the suitability of the facilities available for children of different ages. At primary-school level, the main object is to teach all children to swim before they go on to secondary schools, and in recent years remarkable progress has been made in many areas towards fulfilling this objective.

Realizing that total success cannot be achieved by relying only on the use of public baths or other local pools available for school swimming lessons, forward-looking LEAs have made it their policy to supplement these facilities by encouraging more primary schools to install teaching pools on the premises. These teaching pools constitute the ideal environment for ensuring that as many pupils as possible learn to swim as quickly and easily as possible. Provision of such pools has also been inspired in many cases by the enthusiasm of headteachers, parents, and their friends.

'In practically every case where there is a school pool, 100 per cent of school leavers are swimmers', wrote one director of education; although not all replies to this inquiry put the figure quite as high as that, most certainly suggested that the rate of success measured in terms of leavers able to swim is significantly higher among children who have been taught in their own school pool.

As a rule, confidence in being in the water, essential to a child's first efforts at swimming, cannot easily be gained in the open spaces, intimidating depths, and frequently unsuitable temperatures of the average public bath or lido. Unless newly built with school use in mind, the latter is what its name suggests: a swimming bath for the public, not a pool suitable for teaching children. 'The town pool makes our learners nervous and frightened, so that's why we needed a school pool', as one 11-year-old boy put it in a school essay. Also, although some public baths are available for exclusive use by schools, others have to be shared, with consequent distractions for both teacher and pupils. In this respect, few LEAs are as well served as the city authority whose public facilities include no less than fifteen indoor, heated pools, varying in size from a competition pool to small teaching pools suitable for older infants, and where, the LEA reports, 'for many years the schools have virtually monopolized the use of the baths'.

Second, a school with its own pool is obviously able to provide more children with more swimming lessons, starting at an earlier age and proceeding for a longer period of their primary-school life, than a school dependent on outside facilities. Timetables can be flexible, teaching groups can be of a more convenient size, no time is wasted on travelling, and no money spent on transport and hire charges. In the example quoted above, the county borough education committee reported in 1970 that school use of the public baths was costing more than £30 000 a year. Its total school population is 54 000.

Comments from teachers

Few replies to this inquiry disputed the intrinsic advantages of the school pool. The following quotations are only a few of many comments on the subject from headteachers of schools with their own pools.

> Children are introduced to the water at five years of age and within a few weeks most have overcome their 'fears' . . . Before the pool was built we had swimming only in the summer for the fourth-year classes; now we have it all the year round for everybody. (The pool referred to here is covered and heated.)

> The value to young children of such an amenity is tremendous . . . It allows them to build up confidence in the water for themselves. The pool is shallow enough (about 3 feet) to permit even the smallest or most nervous to stand clear of the surface with comparative ease. As every child in a class will have at least two sessions a week in the pool, a feeling of community is gained in the actual learning situation itself . . .

> We had always been aware that swimming, being an acquired skill, demanded the correct environment at the learning stage if real success

was to be achieved, and we are now convinced that the blessed proximity, the heated water, the privacy, and the ready availability of our pool are providing many of the desired learning conditions. At the same time many peripheral educational and social benefits have been nurtured . . . Every member of the staff and every child in the school can now take part in swimming activities. For many of the staff this is a new setting in which to observe the reactions and behaviour of individual children . . . The children themselves, sensing the security of their very own pool, show . . . little of the apprehension that was occasionally evident in the public bath. The subconscious fear of water which affects a few children is calmed in the familiar closeness of their own heated pool. The smaller teaching groups which are now possible and the consequent increase in individual attention is a further boon for the diffident and for the confident. Learning and practice periods are now infinitely more frequent and administrative timetabling adjustments, necessary to cope with the vagaries of the weather and incidental requests throughout the school, present little difficulty . . .

What the children say

At half past three each Tuesday a bus sets off for the swimming baths . . . There is always a mad scramble for first place on the bus with the boys. Getting out of the bus is bedlam. Everyone pushes out of their seats on to the aisle . . . I have always had butterflies when I go to the baths. The class-eleven boys' clothes are all on the best pegs. You are lucky to get a peg of your own. You get undressed and put your trunks on as quickly as possible. By this time most of my butterflies have died down . . . You wash your knees and line up ready to be called to 'get in'. You jump in and shake off the shivers. Then you start swimming as many widths as you can. When you have done about 40 it is playtime . . . My only good stroke is front crawl. It is very sad when Mr Hutton rings the bell for us to get out. When swimming is over on Tuesday, Tuesday is over too for me.

Our school is very lucky because we go swimming twice a day. We have had our pool for five years. At first we had very few swimmers, for the last two years all our juniors have been able to swim and some of the infants too . . . Our school has twice been a national winner in the Dolphin Trophy and we have won 13 Dolphin Trophy certificates . . . The important part in swimming is to lose fear of water, to get your breathing right, and also to get a good stroke.

III. Patterns of provision

Deciding on a policy of providing more school pools is one thing. Implementing such a policy depends, however, on a number of different factors. These include the type of area, the size and number of schools in it, the geographical distribution of schools in relation to existing swimming facilities, and, above all, the funds available.

There are two main strategies for providing pools. One is to concentrate most funds on permanent concrete installations, even if this means delay in achieving the required amount of expansion. The other is to sacrifice the principle of permanence and equip as many schools as possible as rapidly as possible by investing in prefabricated, plastics-lined portable pools which are relatively inexpensive. These pools are variously referred to as 'liner' pools because of their moulded plastics linings, 'package' pools because the pool lining and other components are delivered to the site as a complete package by manufacturers who offer an inclusive service of design and construction, and 'temporary' pools, although many have a life of five to ten years or more if used carefully. The term 'portable' is used in this report because in the context of school use it most aptly distinguishes this type of pool from its non-portable, permanent counterpart, which is sunk into the ground. It is possible for a portable pool to be wholly or partly sunk into the ground, but most portable, shallow-water teaching pools used in primary schools are free-standing structures with sides above ground level. This means that contact between pupil and teacher is closer and easier for both. Equally important, it means that construction costs are lower than for permanent pools because of reduced expenditure on excavation.

Both strategies are reflected in LEA policies, as was shown in the results of a questionnaire about types of school pools which was sent to approximately one hundred county and county borough authorities. These areas had (in 1970) a total of 1041 portable school pools and 1058 made of permanent concrete. A total of 673 public baths were also being used for school swimming in these areas.

These overall figures conceal striking regional variations in the types of school pools provided, due to the different local needs and circumstances mentioned earlier, as well as to the place given to swimming in an authority's order of priorities, and to the enthusiasm and fund-raising capacities of its headteachers. Funds for school pools are mainly provided by the school community of teachers, pupils, parents, and friends, with a contribution from the LEA. Clearly, therefore, without the development since the early 1950s of relatively inexpensive portable pools to meet the needs of primary schools, countless thousands of children would not have had the chance of learning to swim. In rural areas, where public facilities are often scarce and inaccessible, these pools have played a large part in the expansion of swimming programmes, as can be seen from the figures reported from Kent (108), Cambridgeshire and the Isle of Ely (73), East Sussex (62), Buckinghamshire (57), West Sussex (58), Berkshire (52), Lincolnshire (parts of Lindsey) (43), Wiltshire (29), and Cornwall (19).

In urban areas, too, portable pools installed in spare classrooms can help to relieve the tremendous pressure on public facilities. In 1970 the Inner London Education Authority, for example, had classroom learner pools in 43 primary schools. Elsewhere, playsheds have often been converted to house indoor pools, and other imaginative conversions include old kitchen premises and a Ministry of Works hut.

Permanent concrete pools are more numerous than portable pools in Wales, the Midlands, and the north of England, according to figures in replies from these areas. Authorities with fairly high numbers of this type of pool include Glamorgan (34), Warwickshire (34), Liverpool (32), Leicestershire (27), Durham (25), Shropshire (24), Staffordshire (21), and Coventry (18). These eight authorities had between them only 10 portable school pools but their collective total of public pools was 83.

Whatever the category of pool, there is a wide variety of designs, with costs varying according to size. The following are a few examples, taken from replies that included sufficient relevant details. (The figures of number of pools built and costs relate only to the period up to the summer of 1970 when replies were received.)

Bedfordshire. Since 1964, pools have been installed in 115 out of 141 primary schools and in 6 infants' schools. Most are portable pools. (Although this authority prefers permanent pools, it points out that these call for a contribution from private sources of something like £1000.) Costs range from £776 for the smallest size (16 ft by 16 ft by 26 in) to £1565 for the largest (48 ft by 24 ft by 3 ft). Some permanent concrete pools have also been provided, mostly built as part of a new school within normal limits of cost: about £3000 for the standard primary pool (45 ft by 30 ft by 1½ ft to 3 ft). These pools have a shallow side rather than a shallow end. 'They therefore lend themselves to teaching and the effective use of the whole surface area.'

Devon. Since the first school pool was opened in 1960, there has been a steady annual growth averaging between 15 and 20 pools, bringing the total to more than 150. The majority are prefabricated pools with plastic liners, with a capacity of between 3000 and 10 000 gallons. Seventeen are in permanent concrete.

East Suffolk. Since 1961, pools have been installed in 105 out of 152 primary schools. 'Thirteen of the schools without pools are very small and will be closed within five years, and it is estimated that during this period the remaining 34 schools will have their own pools.' Most pools are of the smaller portable type, 20 ft by 10 ft, costing about £350. Two of the eleven permanent pools in the area were provided at new schools within the normal limits of cost (about £3000), as in Bedfordshire. The chief education officer comments:

> There is considerable merit in being able to dismantle and store a pool on the premises. Winter maintenance is eliminated and costs are reduced to an absolute minimum. From this point of view the portable pool, and particularly the one used in this county, scores heavily. The initial cost is low, maintenance is minimal, in use it is simple, and children learn to swim quickly. For the smaller rural school it is ideal. For the larger school, the permanent pool presents a challenge, but no merit at all is seen in constructing a pool smaller than 30 ft to 40 ft by 15 ft to 20 ft. The aim in East Suffolk is to teach as many children as possible to swim as early as possible. To achieve this every advantage is taken of money immediately available. Mrs Smith is concerned that Johnny learns to swim and not that Johnny's children have a super swimming pool as a result of years of effort and striving during which time Johnny and his contemporaries get no opportunities.

Essex. This county bought the first two plastic-lined Purley pools manufactured in 1958. Both are still in full use. There are now more than 100 school pools in the county, most of them of this type.

Hampshire. About two-thirds of the 44 school pools in the county are made of permanent concrete. The cost of a 40 ft by 20 ft heated outdoor pool of this type varies from £2000 to £3500 including chlorination and filtration plant, paving surroundings, and fencing. The education committee decided, early in the operation of its grants scheme, to give priority to pools of this type, because it was considered that there was at that time insufficient knowledge of the cost of replacement liners for portable pools, maintenance problems, and the life of the fabric. In future, however, it will probably extend its grants scheme to portable pools, which were previously approved only for schools with an uncertain future.

Surrey. Permanent concrete pools account for just over half the county's total of 100 school pools. Most are 50 ft by 15 ft by 3 ft. The remainder are portable pools, generally 42 ft or 48 ft by 16 ft by 3 ft. Costs vary from £600–£700 to £5000–£6000, including filtration and chlorination plant, and with the addition at times of heated and covered buildings. (The authority reports that schools with pools of the dimensions quoted above would appreciate a width nearer to 25 ft.)

Worcestershire. Indoor learner pools, water-heated and made of concrete, are being provided at sixteen key centres throughout the county. They are usually sited in the grounds of large primary schools, each pool serving 12 to 22 smaller schools in its catchment area. Size was increased from 50 ft by 15 ft to 50 ft by 18 ft after the third pool had been built; depth is not more than 3 ft, with a fall only great enough for drainage. Six pools of this type were provided between 1961 and 1968, in which period costs rose from £6000 to £8600. The LEA is meeting the entire cost of these pools.

In other areas, raising the money for pools is almost invariably a co-operative effort involving school communities on the one hand and LEAs on the other. The nature of each kind of contribution, official and voluntary, will be examined in the next chapter.

IV. Raising the money

Just as LEAs pursue different policies about the types of school pools in their areas, so also do they give varying degrees of support to these projects. This support takes a number of forms.

Purchase grants

A grant towards the purchase of the pool is made available, and technical advice on its construction and installation is given by the county architect and other officers. Although the scale of grant aid revealed in the replies ranges from £150 to £1500, most authorities give amounts of the order of 25 or 50 per cent of the purchase price of the pool, up to a limit of £400 or £500, occasionally even £800.

Running costs and maintenance

Further support is given once the pool is built. It then becomes the property of the education committee who take over the responsibility for maintenance and running costs. It is difficult to put an accurate figure to these costs because they vary greatly according to the size and type of pool. One authority reckons that running costs alone vary from £150 a year for a small unheated pool to £400 a year for a heated indoor pool. Another estimates that the total cost of maintenance for each of its indoor learner pools is £250 to £300 a year, of which £150 goes on heating and the rest on general repair and redecoration and the materials used for cleaning or for filtration and chlorination.

Another authority with an exemplary record in this respect comments:

> After the initial expenditure, the schools therefore are relieved of further financial worries. The authority maintains the pool, pays for all running costs, provides all swimming aids, pays for instructors where the permanent staff need this help, and pays for supervisors where the voluntary assistance of parents and friends needs supplementing, especially in school holidays.

18

Maintenance of the pool structure and of the chlorination and filtration plant is the responsibility of the county architect: the quality of
the water that of the public health inspector. They train and supervise
the work of the chlorination and filtration plant operators.

The value of this kind of supportive aftercare is obviously of great
importance with school pools, since the highest standards of water purity
have to be observed, and filtration and chlorination plants must be kept
in efficient working order. (See also 'Filtration and chlorination', p. 25.)

Grants for heating pools and changing-rooms

Money for these purposes usually has to be raised by schools themselves
and by parent–teacher associations, but a small number of authorities
replying to this inquiry also give contributions. In Cambridgeshire, for
example:

> . . . it has now been agreed to grant aid and maintain oil-fired heating
> at a number of schools each year. The use of oil was recommended
> since the maintenance costs are thereby kept to a minimum, the average
> installation cost being approximately £300 for a standard pool of 8000
> gallons. In some cases where the pools are sited close to the school
> boilers it has been possible and cheaper to connect to the existing
> school heating plant. The cost involved in maintaining an average
> water temperature of 70 to 75 throughout a 16 weeks summer and
> early autumn period is approximately £30 to £40.

This authority also makes 50 per cent grants, up to a maximum of £45, to
cover the cost of providing simple changing accommodation, and reports
that 'many schools have taken advantage of this to overcome the problem
of changing for swimming lessons in classrooms or small cloakrooms . . .'

In another area, Hertfordshire, grants of £100 are made towards the
cost of installing heating and also towards the cost of providing changing
accommodation where required; and in Bedfordshire, 'wherever possible
the pool has been connected to the main central heating system, the school
paying for the installation, the authority paying running costs and operating
it from May to September'. (See also 'Covers and heating', pp. 26–8.)
Whatever the degree of support in cash and kind given by LEAs, replies
to this inquiry clearly show that a great many school pools now in existence

would never have been built at all were it not for the determined and dedicated efforts of headteachers supported by their staffs, pupils, and equally determined bands of parents. What these efforts involved in terms of hard work, organization, and community enterprise can best be described in the words of those who provided the inspiration, and this chapter therefore concludes with extracts from some of the impressive accounts sent in by headteachers.

In September 1967 I came to the little school . . . with the delightful Newmarket Racecourse facing us across the main A11 road. The school serves the National Stud and other breeding stables as well as a large farm estate and the Jockey Club. There is no village, only houses scattered around the countryside . . . There were 23 children on roll from 16 families – all except one living in tied cottages on low wages. Having learned the benefits of a swimming pool at my previous school I felt the need here was even greater.

I called a meeting and at least one parent from every family came – we sat round in a circle. I told them we needed a pool and £500 to pay for it. Such a project for a little school naturally stunned them, but they were most enthusiastic and promised full support. I made it clear I didn't want any formal parents' committee but that we should all be in it together. This was readily acceptable and has worked remarkably well. The authority, which usually makes a grant of £250 *after* the balance of money has been raised, delighted us by giving us a 'loan' pool, i.e. they loaned us all the money to begin with. I settled for a 25 foot by 17 foot Purley pool 3 foot deep, which seemed quite big enough for a small school.

The site selected was the only level place on our grass field – even this proved to have a $9\frac{1}{2}$ inch fall . . . It is amazing how much filling is required to level so little slope – 15 tons of it. We then laid paving slabs as a base for the pool to stand on. Most of this work was done by a very few of us since all my fathers are on overtime even at weekends. Here I must pay tribute to a father from my previous school who willingly travelled altogether over 1000 miles to help us . . . Mothers came and painted the sections in the daytime helped by the

1. Concrete sunken pool, showing footbath and changing accommodation.

2. An attractive setting for an outdoor pool. Note the screening.

3. An early example of an inexpensive learner pool.

4. A sectional surface liner pool.

5. Portable pool showing water level lowered for beginners.

6. Mothers helping during a swimming session.

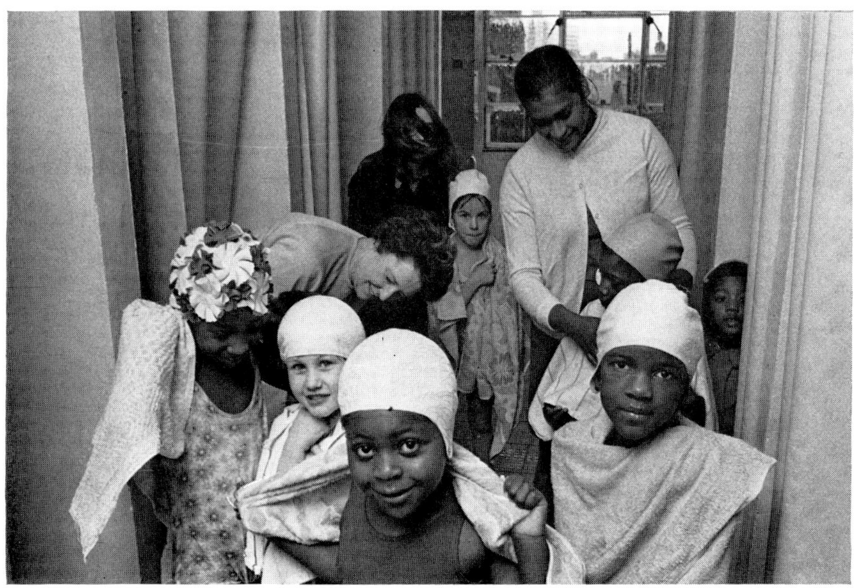

7. Pool covered with translucent sheeting.

8. A portable pool partially covered.

older children. Preparation of the site was the hardest job and in my opinion the most important. The actual erection was completed in one week-end and the pool became operational.

All this time money was being raised by every conceivable means, from selling over 2000 jars of home-made jam and pickles to the usual draws and bingo. The employers connected with the school were remarkably generous . . . Raising the money was the least trouble, over £700 being banked in two years. Last year I decided to go one better and add an infants' pool on the end, as 3 foot deep water is quite impossible for the little ones. We used one end of the pool as one wall of the new pool. We raised the floor so the depth of the water is only 2 feet, though the surface level is the same in both pools. The water circulates through both pools via the filter . . .

We share our pool willingly with a large new primary school in Newmarket whose children come down by bus until their own pool is built. They in turn share their wonderful hall and playing fields with us . . . so the social value of a pool can be most rewarding. The whole project has been colour-filmed as a permanent record of what a small happy family school can achieve – and I hope it will still be shown long after we have been engulfed and disappear under 're-organization'.

.   .   .   .

This is a voluntary controlled junior mixed and infants' school on the north-eastern edge of Harlow New Town. The school is fortunate in having children from a wide range of social backgrounds and although there is no parent–teacher association we are lucky to have excellent relationships with our parents. At the end of 1960 it was decided to build a school swimming pool . . . Both staff and parents were enthusiastic. Among the parents we had carpenters, plumbers, painters and electricians, an urban district engineer to plan and level the site, a doctor to advise on health hazards and a multitude of willing diggers . . . We decided on a Purley pool 41 feet by 25 feet; at the time it seemed best value for money and now there appears no real reason for regretting the decision. We are at present on our tenth season and it has been necessary to renew the plastic lining only once, after about five years use. The wood surround has stood the test of time well.

Work started at the same time as fund-raising. With the help of a grant from the Essex County Council we collected sufficient money in less than six months to pay for the pool itself and a filtration plant housed in its own small hut. In fact the pool was in use by mid-June 1961 and we had no financial worries.

A changing hut was added to the site in 1964; a gas-fired boiler, installed in April 1967, meant a lengthening of the swimming season. The county council provided an excellent wooden fence to enclose the site. Swimming is now a well-established part of the school curriculum and from the beginning of the summer term until well into October most of the juniors swim daily, the infants two or three times a week . . . We take the view that as a school housed in rather antiquated buildings with fairly poor facilities for indoor PE we are right to use our swimming pool as much as possible during the better weather; we are sure the children agree!

   .   .   .   .

At the appointment of a new headteacher, a parents' meeting was called . . . and a parent–teacher association was formed in October 1963. At its first meeting, unanimous support was given to raise money towards a swimming pool. Plans for various money-raising functions were made and within six months the first children were swimming in our Mermaid (10 000 gallons) pool. With PTA money and a 50 per cent grant from the county, the school had a pool that its civic leaders had hoped for in 1939!

The pool, filter, and fencing around the pool cost approximately £700. Within 12 months further extensions had been made to incorporate changing facilities attached to the site . . . All the surrounds of the pool and changing cubicles are now concrete-paved. With these extensions and other equipment provided the total cost would amount to £1000, £750 of which has been raised by the PTA.

In addition to the normal school-time swimming, out-of-school clubs also make use of the pool . . . To ensure even more use of the pool, parents now swim on three evenings a week. This is run entirely by parents and a nominal charge of 5p per evening is charged. This money is being used for further developments (covering and heating?).

All of these examples relate to portable pools, but in some areas schools have also tackled the more ambitious and expensive task of installing permanent pools. Illustrations of two very different but equally successful ways of raising money for these costly projects were provided by two schools in the same seaside area.

The total cost of their permanent heated concrete pools was £3500 and £3875 respectively, and an LEA grant of £450 was made for each. Even without this help, School A organized fund-raising activities ranging from jumble sales to sponsored walks so successfully that £3500 was raised and the pool opened within fourteen months of starting.

School B pioneered an entirely new approach, formulated by the treasurer of its PTA, so as to avoid the arduous work of fund-raising over a long period in which, because of rising costs, the original target figure often has to be raised. 'Build first – pay later' is the theme of this new approach. A bank loan was obtained on the strength of covenanted sub-scriptions from parents, and the pool was in use six months after the scheme was launched. It will be paid for within seven years 'without a single fête or money-raising effort being held.'

For the benefit of other schools who might wish to adopt a scheme of this kind, the headteacher's account of it appears as Appendix A.

V. Essentials and extras

Whatever type of school pool may be chosen, a number of additional items have to be reckoned with in planning its installation. Some, like a cleansing plant, are obviously essential; others, like covers to lengthen the swimming season, are optional extras which some schools feel they must have, while others prefer to concentrate their resources elsewhere. For example, one LEA in the west of England said it would prefer to spend money on building more school pools than use the limited funds available on heating and covering existing pools. In contrast, the headmaster of a Yorkshire school with an open-air pool has organized fund-raising for a £2700 building to cover the pool and give protection against 'the inevitable cool sea breeze cropping up after lunch'.

The essentials and extras listed in this chapter are in the nature of an aide-mémoire and are certainly not a comprehensive guide to the items under discussion. To avoid the pitfalls often involved in building a school pool, and to advise on the best choice of equipment for different needs from among the wide variety available on the market, one or two enterprising LEAs produce booklets for schools wishing to install pools. One county education committee (Somerset) publishes an admirable series of informative guides covering every aspect from the pool itself to construction, siting, water purification, costs, covers, and heating. Such booklets can be highly recommended and for anyone planning to embark on a school pool building project, it would be well worth while to find out first whether published information is also available in their area. One example of the kind of expensive mistake that can occur when advice is not sought was provided by a school that spent £300 on a cleansing plant which proved totally inadequate for the required bathing load and had to be replaced by a new plant costing twice as much. Even if technical advice is not available in the form of the booklets mentioned above, it can always be obtained from the health department of the LEA and the county architect's office.

Filtration and chlorination

For school pools with their heavy bathing loads, it is naturally of crucial importance to maintain the highest standards of water purity at all times to prevent the spread of infection. This means, first, investing in really efficient filtration and chlorination plants that are capable of coping with the envisaged bathing load.

Chlorination is sometimes carried out by hand, particularly in smaller pools, but an automatic plant is generally considered more advisable. The headmaster of a school where the pool was manually chlorinated for several years found this method 'time-consuming, wasteful of materials, and at times impossible to maintain the health standard required', and recommended installing automatic continuous chlorination from the outset.

Daily water checks are necessary, and although usually carried out by school caretakers or groundsmen, these checks need to be supervised by the head or a member of the staff; they in turn can call for advice from the county medical officer's department who will also make regular, routine inspections of pool water as part of the local authority's arrangements for aftercare and maintenance of school pools. (See Chapter IV.)

Good practice in this respect means that the person responsible, instructed by the county medical department, checks the water two or three times a day for pH value and chlorine. He carries out the chlorination process, cleans the pool surrounds, cleans the footbath and refills it with a disinfecting solution, and backwashes the filtration plant. In addition, sampling officers from the health department at county hall regularly visit each school pool during the swimming season to make check tests. Some LEAs supplement these arrangements by organizing conferences on water treatment, maintenance, and equipment which are attended by teachers and school caretakers.

Footbaths and lavatories

Personal hygiene is of the greatest importance in school swimming, both as a matter of principle and because water purity can be greatly affected by the amount of contamination taken into a pool by bathers. Schools should always enforce the use of lavatories and footbaths before entering the water as a matter of routine. Footbaths should be sited so that it is impossible to enter the water without first going through the footbath and then straight into the pool. The footbath should be designed so that it can be cleaned and drained easily, and it should be regularly replenished with fresh water and disinfecting solution. One of the LEA guides mentioned earlier in this chapter recommends one fluid ounce of sodium hypochlorite to four gallons of water for disinfecting footbaths. If showers are not available, children should have a quick wash before swimming.

Paving, fencing, handrails, and steps

Paving surrounds rather than grass are important in contributing to pool hygiene. Grass can quickly become a soggy mess, with clippings drifting into the water. If paving is too expensive, pebbles provide a cheaper alternative.

Fencing is obviously highly desirable. It gives a feeling of privacy and security, keeps out wind-blown debris, and helps to raise the water temperature. One expert authority maintains that seasonal use of an outdoor pool can be extended by one month where there is a fence. Handrails to assist children entering the pool and for teaching swimming strokes, as well as permanent or portable steps and, where appropriate, an inclined slope for handicapped children, complete the list of essential pool-building accessories.

Covers and heating

Although most schools have heated pools so that swimming can go on from May until the end of September, comparatively few have the advantage of a covered pool in which swimming can continue throughout the year. Several makes of permanent pool covers or enclosures are available, but the prices – ranging from about £1500 to £3000 – are enough to daunt even the most vigorous PTAs. A less expensive enclosure, providing partial cover, was the subject of one or two favourable reports. One authority's PE adviser described it as 'a very successful shelter for the price . . . the open roof helps to prevent the formation of condensation at any time. Temperature readings show an 8–9 degrees improvement between the outside air and that inside the shelter at any time.' This

26

enclosure for an average-sized pool cost £600–£800 and was erected with the help of parents.

Another method of obtaining cover for smaller pools is by utilizing an existing building such as a playshed or spare classroom. The cost of converting classrooms and installing pools was estimated in replies at £1400 to £1800, depending on size and type of construction. Elsewhere, a pool 24 ft by 16 ft was housed in a covered play area, requiring the construction of walls on two sides to enclose it, at a total cost of £2000, and playshed installations were variously costed at between £800 and £1240.

Finally, mention must be made of a remarkably enterprising solution by the headmaster of a primary school in Essex, who designed a cover for his 52 ft by 16 ft pool and built it with the help of a few parents at a total cost of approximately £300. Here are a few extracts from his account.

> Faced with the problem of covering our pool when it became obvious that a pool, unless covered, is lying idle for nine months of the year, I decided to design and construct one myself.
>
> Our problem was cash; we had no PTA and there were only 65 children on the roll. However, the whole project – swimming pool, filter, heater, cover, and polystyrene blocks for keeping in the heat – only cost £1000, and this was raised and the pool and cover completed in two years.
>
> Method of construction: There was already a concrete surround. On this concrete blocks were cemented. These blocks had spaces in them into which bolts were cemented at intervals of five feet. To those were bolted steel ribs. These were rusty, second-hand, Nissen-hut ribs which had to be de-rusted and then treated with a special rust-proof paint. It would be nearly as cheap to hot-dip galvanise them, and certainly better, although after seven years there are only very faint rust spots here and there.
>
> On to these steel ribs we fastened wooden purlins, which we had pre-drilled to the same measurements, to keep the building square. The steel ribs also had to be drilled while on the ground and bolted together. There are five pieces to a semi-circle.
>
> Finally, PVC sheeting was nailed to the wooden purlins. The sheeting first had to be drilled in situ as it has to be overlapped and there are four thicknesses at each corner. The ends were then filled in, in the

same manner, care being taken to let the wind blow through until on the final day both ends were completed.

Bearing in mind condensation troubles, we fitted double doors at both ends, flanked by two windows on either side. Thus there was plenty of ventilation and of course if condensation was a bother, suction fans could have been inserted. Finally four steel hawsers were fitted at each corner with a tightening device to keep the whole building rigid.

Total cost was approximately £300, but 50 per cent discount was obtained on the sheeting, which was the costliest item; the material is now a good deal cheaper. Maintenance costs to the building are about £35 for the seven years.

The cover has meant all-year-round swimming (which I believe is essential) and does help to keep fuel costs down. With a cover such as this, the interior does not need heating except in winter, and in summer will keep the water at 70° F without using the heat. In winter, water temperature is kept at 80° F . . .

It must be remembered that the cost was for materials only. The labour was provided by myself and a few parents. This design has now been used by three other schools, although a great many have come to look . . . During the last two years we have been a national winner for the Dolphin Trophy twice . . .

Finally, mention should be made of a completely different kind of cover for conserving water heat. For unheated pools, these light covers, generally made of plastic sheeting, can be recommended to prevent heat loss during the night.

VI. Teaching swimming

'There is no mystique about the teaching of swimming', wrote one head-teacher. Another quoted the comment of a class teacher: 'In no other form of teaching do you see your results so quickly.'

A few local authorities employ instructors to help with swimming lessons at school, but in the great majority of areas covered by this inquiry lessons are taken by the class teacher. 'The enthusiasm of teachers is unbounded', wrote one LEA, 'although many start with only a limited knowledge of stroke technique and methods of group teaching. For this reason courses for teachers, which are very well supported, are run at regular intervals in different parts of the county, and the physical education advisers give help on their visits to schools.' Progress made in turning out competent primary-school swimmers, 'would not have been possible without the co-operation of so many teachers', said another LEA which also runs short in-service courses to help teachers gain confidence in simple methods of teaching swimming in small surface pools as well as modern methods of resuscitation. A number of LEAs run these courses, often in conjunction with the Amateur Swimming Association.

At public pools, paid instructors are usually provided by LEAs. Class teachers invariably go with their pupils to these pools and frequently share the work with the instructors.

In all types of pool, classes are normally limited to twenty children with one teacher. The exceptions are the small school learner pools, where it is common for groups of about eight children to have a lesson at one time.

In both cases, this often gives rise to problems of supervision of the remaining half waiting for their turn in the water, but different schools have worked out their solutions to this 'split class' difficulty. In some areas, the 'second teacher' is the headteacher; in others, school helpers are used or swimming instructors imported for the purpose. Elsewhere, headteachers often report that mothers have willingly come to school on a rota basis to help supervise one half of a class while the rest are swimming. Frequently, too, mothers go to school at swimming time to help younger children to dry and dress. In some of the areas where lessons take place in public baths, the group of children waiting for their turn to swim can usefully observe the rest of the class having instruction in the water.

Timetabling of swimming lessons naturally varies according to the facilities being used. Schools with their own pools are able to provide several lessons a week, and often a daily lesson. For those using public baths, one lesson a week lasting up to half an hour is the usual ration. Serial teaching is generally preferred when outside pools are used, because this fits in more easily with the curriculum, but one or two LEAs reported successful and continuing experiments in combining block and serial methods to get the best possible results. In the Inner London Education Authority area, where junior-schoolchildren generally swim at public baths once a week for a year, special intensive courses are arranged each summer at about six centres. 'Children in their last year at primary school who have not yet learned to swim are offered the opportunity of a daily lesson for three weeks. These special arrangements have proved success- ful in enabling a number of persistent non-swimmers to become water- borne, indeed some have become quite accomplished swimmers in the three weeks course.'

This comment was echoed by the headmaster of a school with its own pool, who believes that lessons:

> need to be as close together as possible, so that children do not forget or have time to lose any confidence they have gained. A daily lesson is the ideal but, from my experience, if a class of children of 7-plus are given ten or twelve lessons over a period of three weeks, only the very nervous children will fail to swim. Holiday courses arranged on these lines, for some 400 children aged 7 to 11, have given a success rate of 90 per cent or over.

Although teaching methods vary to some extent according to the teacher, the basic routines mentioned in most reports accord with the following summary provided by one LEA:

> *Beginners.* Use of artificial aids of all types. Water-confidence work in game-like situations. Some personal survival techniques of an elementary kind.
>
> *Mixed ability.* Group teaching. A continuation of water-confidence work, with more specific coaching of strokes being gradually intro-

duced. Generally speaking, multi-stroke methods are used, though some teachers prefer to build up a single stroke.

Swimmers. Coaching of strokes. Personal survival work and different methods of entry (jumping, plunging, and diving) may be introduced in pools of suitable depth.

The importance of maintaining children's water-confidence was emphasized in several reports. As one headteacher wrote:

At all stages it is most important that nothing happens which will destroy the child's confidence. Pushing in or ducking should be strictly prohibited; aids must be securely fitted – losing balance and floundering in the water can be a frightening experience which will certainly retard progress considerably.

Another vital consideration, whether children swim in a school pool or in a public bath, is the observance of certain elementary safety precautions. These are usefully summarized in notes issued by one education committee to all its schools, which include the following points:

1. Whenever children are in the water, whether shallow or deep, there should be a responsible person teaching or supervising from the bath side – either a teacher or the baths instructor.

2. If the teacher or instructor wishes to enter the water to teach, there must be another responsible person on the bath side to watch the rest of the class. This responsible person should be prepared (and suitably clothed) to enter the water if necessary to assist a child in difficulties.

3. In swimming baths with deep water the teacher or instructor in charge of the group must be a competent swimmer.

4. Schools with their own pool should have available at all times in a handy place a long bamboo pole or other suitable aid.

5. Teachers taking children to public baths should make certain that they know where safety equipment is kept.

6. A suitable number of children to be in the charge of one teacher, supervisor, or instructor is 20. Under no circumstances should there be more than 30.

7. Running round the bath, either before or during the lesson, can be dangerous.

(It should be added here it is desirable for teachers to be familiar with modern methods of resuscitation, a subject covered in the courses for teachers run by many LEAs which were referred to earlier in this chapter.)

Most reports from LEAs and schools stress the importance of graded proficiency tests, certificate awards, and other schemes in helping teachers to check progress, and encouraging children to improve their abilities. One of the LEAs quoted above distributes over 10 000 certificates each year to primary-school pupils in the county:

> A teacher with special interest in swimming is appointed in each of twelve areas to make arrangements for testing and issuing certificates. These teachers meet annually with the county advisers for physical education, so that the scheme itself, its practical operation and the standard of testing, is kept under constant review. In view of the increasing number of national certificate schemes now available for this age group, the question has arisen recently whether it is now time to abandon the county scheme. It may be interesting to note, however, that teachers have reported an overwhelming desire to retain the county scheme, in which modifications can easily and quickly be made to suit local conditions.

This authority and others report that teachers give up a great deal of their free time, often during the holidays, to work on schemes like this, and take a keen interest in the progress made by children in their area.

Elsewhere, besides taking certificates for distance, stroke proficiency, and simple diving, children are encouraged to take the various safety tests available, such as the personal survival awards of the Amateur Swimming Association. In addition, many schools devise their own awards for testing confidence and ability.

What the children say

> The first thing we learnt was to get our heads under water. One of the ways we did this was by playing games like a ring of roses and when we came to the 'all fall down' bit, that made us put our heads under the water. In no time at all we were used to the idea. At the end of the first year we could all swim quite well on our backs. In the second year we were taught the front crawl and the breast stroke. We also did some floating practice and swimming under water . . . In the third

year we started to practise diving, both sitting and racing dives. That year I went on a swimming course where we took distance tests . . . In the fourth year we did revision of all the strokes we had learnt, diving as well. My favourite stroke is front crawl.

. . . .

Before I was in the juniors I was unable to swim, then the teachers tried to teach us and I still couldn't until they introduced me to swimming bands. These are like rubber rings except you put them on your arms. When I was little I had many fears about going under the water and many, many other things. But now I only have two. One in which I would hate to dive, and two, I would hate to be pushed under and kept there.

VII. The future

In an ideal world, facilities for teaching children to swim would be plentiful and perfect for every age group: glorified paddling pools for infants, shallow-water teaching pools for the early years at primary school, deeper pools for older juniors who have learned to swim, and so on up the scale of developing abilities.

Until recently, however, swimming facilities in this country have developed in a fairly piecemeal, haphazard fashion rather than as the result of conscious planning to meet properly researched needs. Thus several reports spoke of the need for children who have acquired confidence and competence in shallow-water school teaching pools to have carefully supervised opportunities for developing their skills in the unaccustomed environment of larger areas of water. In some parts, this need can be met, and is met, by taking older juniors on regular visits to public pools or to those of neighbouring secondary schools. In other areas where primary schools have striven successfully to produce a high proportion of leavers who can swim, further progress may be in danger of being halted by a lack of convenient facilities for further development.

Fortunately there is now an increasing tendency for local authorities and education authorities to co-operate in planning swimming facilities suitable for teaching as well as for adult recreation. School pools can provide admirable examples of this concept of dual use. Many are used by the community at large, including the parents who often helped to build them. The interest of parents in these projects has the further benefit that it may, and often does, lead to a wider understanding of school life as a whole, and of the problems and principles of education.

Appendices

Appendix A 'Build first – pay later':
a new approach to fund-raising

By the headteacher of a primary school

The over-riding factor that deters many schools from launching a campaign to provide the necessary finance with which to build a swimming pool is the seemingly never-ending money-raising activities that have to be undertaken. These must inevitably, despite the very best of intentions, cause a varying measure of disruption in a school. A tremendous amount of work is involved, and while in the early stages enthusiasms run high, these soon dwindle, and the whole project can become extremely arduous. Another factor to be considered is the rise in costs while the money is being raised. More often than not, the original target figure has to be considerably increased.

Because of these reasons, as headteacher of a new and small school, I had to resist the enthusiasm of a number of parents who wished to launch such a scheme, until an entirely new approach to the idea was formulated by the treasurer of our parent–teacher association. This was later adopted at a meeting of parents and for the benefit of any who might care to consider adopting a similar approach to the problem a simplified outline of the scheme is given here.

We sought and were granted permission by the Commissioners of Inland Revenue, Charities Division, to establish a trust fund for the school. A trust deed had to be prepared, setting out the aims of the trust, and it should be remembered at this point that such a trust cannot have one particular aim, i.e. the provision of a swimming pool, but that the aims must be more general such as the provision of further amenities for the school, etc.

We also inquired of the Department of Education and Science whether this was permissible in a state primary school. We were readily given permission and told that, although as far as they knew we were the first primary school to attempt such a scheme, it was a noteworthy venture and that they would be interested to know the result.

This then enabled us to invite parents to covenant subscriptions to the trust fund. This has several distinct advantages. Each subscription is increased by approximately 70 per cent due to the recovery of tax from the Inland Revenue. Thus if the total subscriptions received in one year under deed of covenant amount to £300, approximately a further £210 will be added when the tax is recovered from the Inland Revenue, bringing the total to £510. A deed of covenant must run for seven years – a slight disadvantage that I shall refer to later. Accordingly, if £510 is multiplied by seven, it will be seen that a basic subscription income of £300 per year will achieve a grand total of £3570 in seven years – a formidable target to achieve by traditional methods in the same time.

On the strength of the covenants we were able to secure a bank loan, and the contractors commenced building at the earliest possible date. Our scheme was launched in the spring of 1969. Children were swimming in September of the same year, the specialist contractors taking only six weeks to complete the pool.

We did feel that as a deed of covenant must run for seven years, many parents would not wish to agree to this form of undertaking, especially as their particular children were only to be in the school for a few years longer. We were, however, very pleasantly surprised at how many parents appreciated that even if their children were only to have one or two years use of the pool, it was a worth-while investment.

Our pool is 25 ft × 50 ft × 3 ft. It is of permanent construction, part raised and part sunk, and the gross cost, including heating and filtration plant, was £3875. The local authority gave a grant of £450 and this, together with the covenanted subscriptions plus the recovery of tax, plus a few ordinary uncovenanted subscriptions, has raised £1507 in the first year.

As new children join the school, their parents are invited to join the scheme and many of them do so. Thus our belief that it would 'snowball' is being borne out.

We were very fortunate to have among our parents professional men who have dealt with the financial, legal, and architectural matters, which might otherwise have involved professional fees.

36

When the pool has been paid for, the intention is then to build dressing-rooms, adjoining the pool and equipped with showers, which can also be used for games purposes. Following that, we may possibly cover in the pool.

The amount suggested to parents as an annual subscription was £3. Quite a few offered more, and some less. If the area is a reasonably affluent one, this is an excellent way of raising money for such a scheme; but it should be remembered that the essential thing is to persuade people to covenant subscriptions because of the tremendous help given through the recovery of tax, and because this will also help persuade the bank to provide a loan.

If we, a small school, can do this, a larger school should find it proportionately easier. I thoroughly recommend 'having a go'.

Appendix B   Useful addresses

Amateur Swimming Association
Acorn House
314 Grays Inn Road
London WC1

British Association of Organisers and Lecturers in Physical Education
Education Offices
Park Road
Hartlepool
Co. Durham

Central Council for Physical Recreation
160 Great Portland Street
London W1N 5TB

English Schools Swimming Association
190 Nether Street
West Finchley
London N3

Institute of Baths Management
256a Green Lanes
Palmers Green
London N13

National Playing Fields Association
57b Catherine Place
London SW1

Physical Education Association of Great Britain and Northern Ireland
10 Nottingham Place
London W1

Royal Life Saving Society
14 Devonshire Street
London W1

RoSPA (Royal Society for the Prevention of Accidents)
52 Grosvenor Gardens
London SW1

Sports Council
26 Park Crescent
London W1

Swimming Pool and Allied Trades Association Ltd
87 London Road
Croydon CRO 2RF

Swimming Teachers Association
Queens College Chambers
38a Paradise Street
Birmingham 1

Technical Unit for Sport
Department of Education and Science
Elizabeth House
York Road
London SE1

Welsh Amateur Swimming Association
45 Devon Place
Newport
Mon

Welsh Physical Education Association
Wenallt
20 Brynmawr Place
Maesteg
Glam

Welsh Schools Swimming Association
(Secretary: J. T. Butler)
Yr Hafod Wen
Trenwle Court
Treorci
Rhondda
Glam